SkillsWork

Teacher's Book

Lynda Edwards

Contents

Introduction

Unit notes

The Teacher's Notes for *SkillsWork* include a summary of what each unit contains, ideas for lead in activities, suggested lesson procedure, extra activities for each unit and an answer key. The main structure and features of each lesson are outlined below.

Summary

The summary at the top of each page will let you know several things about that particular unit. You can see at a glance what topics are covered and the type of associated vocabulary work done. You can also see the main and subsidiary tasks for the unit. The focus skill is given at the top of the page but each unit also includes work on linked skills.

Warmer

A suggested warmer is given for each unit. This should be done before the books are opened to establish the concept of the unit in as natural a way as possible. The warmers given have been designed not to overlap any other points that might be raised or covered in that particular unit.

Procedure

The rubrics in the Student's Book should make the setting up of tasks clear. Naturally the procedure will vary depending on time, need, and interest among other things. You may wish to cut out some activities, reorder, change pair work to group work, etc. The procedure given is suggested only.

Extra activities

There is an additional activity provided for each unit, and sometimes there is more than one. This can be used to supplement the tasks in the unit or occasionally to replace them. The extra activities include lexical, speaking and written work. It may sometimes be necessary for you to dictate the task or write it on the board.

Key

The answer key is given at point of use, not at the end of the book.

Timing

Timing of tasks depends on the needs of the groups. The aim is to maintain variety and balance so that the students are continually engaged in what they are doing. If a discussion in a speaking skills focus lesson is going very well, involving all students, it could take up the best part of the lesson. The activities in a lesson do not all have to be 'done' simply because they are there in the book.

Activity types

There is a wide range of activity type in the book. All should be suitable for young adults and adults. Many of the activity types are seen in exams and can provide useful practice. The topics are also wide ranging and cover subjects of interest to all of us.

Tapescripts

The tapescript is at the back of the Student's Book so it can easily be accessed by the students for lexical and pronunciation work as well as comprehension checking.

Classroom management

Pairs or groups?

Many of the activities in *SkillsWork* are set up as pairwork. This is because in theory pairwork means students have maximum talking time. However, depending on your class, it may well be more appropriate to put students in small groups – particularly when you want them to come up with a range of ideas. It is usually a good idea to give students time in pairs or groups to get their thoughts together before putting them on the spot as a class. Ensuring variety and balance in pairings is important to maintain interest. Good pairing can also help avoid problems with students who either have a tendency to dominate or withdraw. Knowing who to pair comes from knowing the class and understanding the personalities. It is certainly worth taking the trouble to plan the pairing and groupings as this can have a significant affect on the success of a lesson.

Feedback

After a pairwork or small group work activity try to allow time for at least some feedback. This gives a point to the work they have done. Don't insist that every student contributes as this will become tedious. Instead vary the students you ask for feedback.

Discussion

It is important in discussions not to allow a few students to dominate. Be aware of the students who have something to say and help them into the discussion by directing questions at these specific individuals. If appropriate, the teacher can contribute. This makes the discussion real for the students. Watch out for the moment that the discussion begins to flag. When this happens, wind the discussion up and move on rather than let the motivation and enthusiasm wane. It is also possible that the discussion may take on a life of its own and go in an unexpected direction. As long as all students are involved and engaged, it is often good practice to allow this to happen and not feel tied to your lesson plan. This is much easier to do in a skills lesson than when following a regular coursebook lesson.

Monitoring

It is important to be aware of what is happening in pair and group work without inhibiting the students. Initial monitoring will ensure that the students are doing the right things and have understood the task correctly. The amount of interaction the teacher has while monitoring will obviously depend on the type of task. If a pair is having problems coming up with ideas, they can be prompted. If a task is going well there may be no need to interact at all. In a skills lesson the monitoring stage is not usually appropriate for detailed correction unless the students are misusing lexis in a vocabulary practice task. However, it is useful to make a mental note of any repeated errors which might be worth checking with the whole class later on in the lesson. It is not always a good idea to physically note these down while monitoring as it can inhibit the less confident students. It is important to at least walk round the class while they are working in pairs or small groups. Students generally like to know that the teacher is involved and concerned about what they are doing rather than sitting at the desk marking essays while they are talking.

Correction

The level of correction necessary during a discussion or speaking activity is always difficult to gauge. On the one hand, the teacher doesn't want to bring a promising discussion to a halt by overcorrecting while the students are talking. On the other, the students like to feel that their mistakes are not going completely unnoticed. It is a delicate balance as every teacher knows. One answer is to make sure that students know the difference between a fluency and accuracy activity and that with fluency activities you will not be correcting during the activity but with accuracy activities you obviously will.

Vocabulary

There is a significant amount of new lexis in *SkillsWork*. Much of the vocabulary is dealt with in *Word work* tasks but you may need to pre-teach some words and expressions for the listenings and readings, depending on the level of your class. Always try to recycle new vocabulary and check how much students can remember. It is often a good idea to have students test each other. Vocabulary testing can be done in many ways including gap fills, dictation, pronunciation practice, etc. Check students understand the level of

formality of new vocabulary. There are many tasks on this in the book but it is always a good idea to make it clear to students which words or expressions can be used when, where and with whom! When clarifying the meaning of new lexis, try to make your explanation clear and memorable. Definitions will only work with easy words and don't help students remember the meanings. Give interesting examples and always put the new words into context – or get the students to do this. This serves as a double check. You can see that the students have correctly understood the meaning and demonstrated that they know how to use it.

Writing tasks

Writing tasks are used for different reasons with different classes. Writing tasks can be an opportunity to consolidate language items learned in a particular lesson. They also give students invaluable practice of a skill that they may need in the future – for work, examinations or social correspondence. By this stage students will be well aware that the language of writing is very different to that of speaking and that care and time need to be spent on a piece of writing. Encourage preparation and planning to guide them through the tasks. They should also be aware of differences in register and the importance of spelling, punctuation, sentence structure and paragraphing. Proof reading is a good skill for students to develop – either of their own work or another's (where appropriate). Where time does not allow students to complete the written work in class, the tasks can be done at home. Correction techniques are down to individual teachers and their students' needs and expectations. A class that is working towards an examination will need a lot of correction and guidance in their written work. However, be aware that overcorrection can destroy the confidence of a hesitant student.

Lesson notes

See pages 6 and 7 for suggestions on how to plan lessons.

Lesson notes

These photocopiable pages can be used as an aid for skills lessons using *SkillsWork*. This is not a traditional 'lesson plan' but more of an opportunity to note down things to remember or check during, before or after the lesson.

WARMER
Supplementary materials/props

Notes on current relevance: recent events, articles, news stories

LEAD IN
Additional questions/activity

WORD WORK
Difficult items

Definitions

Alternative contexts

Examples

Extra activities

ACTIVITIES
Pairs

Back up activity for students who finish early

Notes during monitoring

Notes during discussion

Questions to redirect discussion

Which activity to leave out if lesson overruns

LANGUAGE CHECK
How to check/test new language at end of lesson

HOMEWORK
What to set for homework

POST LESSON NOTES
What needs further practice/recycling

What worked well and why

What to avoid in future and why

Need some company?

Summary

Topic: being alone

Vocabulary: word building; colloquial expressions; asking for opinions

Main task: interactive picture based discussion

Subsidiary tasks: discussion; writing an email

Warmer

Write the word *alone* on the board and elicit from the class whether it has negative, positive or neutral connotations.

Write the words *loneliness* and *solitude* below it and ask how these relate to what has been said.

Procedure

Lead in

Students discuss questions in pairs. Feed back and compare answers with the class.

Word work

1 a Students do word building activity. Check answers and give examples where necessary.

Key

Possible answers

alone: lone   lonely   loneliness   a loner
solitude: sole   solitary
isolate: isolated   isolation
company: companion   companionable   companionship
society: sociable   unsociable   social   socially   associate   association

b Students complete task in pairs. Check answers. Elicit contexts for the collocations.

Key

1 sole beneficiary   **2** isolation ward
3 solitary confinement   **4** unsociable hours
5 keep someone company

2 a Set matching task as individual work. Check answers.

Key

1 d   **2** e   **3** a   **4** c   **5** h   **6** f   **7** b   **8** g

b Students work in pairs to divide expressions. Check answers.

Key

A 1 3 5 6   **B** 2 4 7 8

3 Ask students to provide contexts for expressions individually. Feed back and compare answers with the class.

Talk about it

1 a Elicit correct alternatives in open group.

b  **1.1** Play the recording for students to repeat. Focus on intonation and contractions.

2 Monitor students as they discuss the question in pairs. Elicit feedback and extend discussion.

3 Students discuss questions in pairs or small groups and feed back.

Write about it

Set writing task in class or for homework.

Extra activity

Write this rubric on the board.

> Many problems in the world today are caused by having too many people. Here are some of them.
>
> - overpopulation
> - large classroom sizes
> - larger retired population
> - overcrowding in large cities
> - more single parents
>
> Talk to each other about the causes and potential effects of these problems and then decide which you think is the most worrying problem.

Set the task as pair work. Feed back. Discuss with students what they think could be done to ease these problems.

What's in a voice?

Summary

Topic: voices; advertising

Vocabulary: adjectives to describe voice and manner

Main task: listening to radio adverts for gist and detailed information

Subsidiary tasks: discussion; intonation work; writing an advert

Warmer

If you know the class, greet them with a smile but no words. Write *Can you describe my voice?* on the board.

Elicit with gestures and write any adjectives or comments on the board. If you don't know the class, ask them to describe a particular student's voice.

Ask the student to speak and see how appropriate the descriptions were.

Elicit from students what they could consider when describing a voice and write these words on the board for reference: *pitch*, *tone*, *pace*, *clarity*, *intonation*, *accent*.

Procedure

Lead in

Students discuss questions in pairs. Feed back and compare answers as a class.

Listen

 **2.1** Ask different students to read the sentence. Then play the recording for students to match adjectives and speakers. Check answers.

Key
1 gossipy   2 sexy   3 business-like   4 nasal
5 squeaky   6 hesitant

Word work

1 Students work on adjectives in pairs, referring to their dictionaries if necessary. Check answers as a class. There may be some discussion about which answers are correct as the classification of some of the words is a matter of opinion.

Key
Positive: husky, smooth, sexy, clear, gentle, strong, musical, hypnotic, warm, deep, soft, friendly, enthusiastic, rich

Negative: irritating, incomprehensible, strongly-accented, nasal, piercing, aggressive, whining, sharp, loud, squeaky, nervous, pompous
Neutral: high, fast business-like, gossipy, hesitant, upper class

2 Students think of people's voices individually and compare answers in pairs. Feed back as a class

3 Students work in pairs to practise saying the sentence in different ways.

Listen

1 Students discuss pre listening questions in open group.

2 Students discuss questions in pairs. Feed back.

3 Before playing the recording, check tapescript and preteach any unfamiliar items. Set listening task as individual work then students check in pairs. Play the recording. Check answers as a class. Note that answers for the tone may vary.

Key

advert	product	name	tone
1	chocolates	Moonlight Magic	sexy
2	carpets	Carpet Stores	enthusiastic
3	shampoo/conditioner	Revelle 5	gentle, warm
4	washing powder	Whitestar	complaining/ reassuring
5	car	Panther	husky/sexy
6	insurance	Insurance Direct	business-like

4 Students discuss how successful they think the adverts would be. Compare ideas as a class.

Write about it

Students prepare writing task in small groups. If there is not enough time, ask students to write the script for homework.

Extra activity

1 Read this paragraph in different ways (enthusiastic/ unenthusiastic). Ask students what differences they notice.

> Went out to dinner with John again last night. He brought his sister along. She sat next to me and told me all about her holiday house in the south of France. 'You must come and stay sometime,' she said. 'I'm sure we could fit you in.'

2 Write these sentences for students to practise saying with different intonation. Model if necessary to check.

> 1 I love your hippy look. Are the clothes original? (admiration/sarcasm)
> 2 Their taste in decorating is incredible. (praise/shock)
> 3 I see you finished late again last night. (worry/criticism)

Common sense

Summary

Topic: Telepathy

Vocabulary: words with similar meanings; expressions for giving opinions

Main task: reading a newspaper article; answering multiple choice questions

Subsidiary tasks: discussion; giving opinions; writing a paragraph giving an opinion

Warmer

Write *SENSES?* on the board and elicit the five senses from students.

Ask students what their favourite and least favourite smells/tastes/sounds etc are.

Procedure

Lead in

Students answer the questions in pairs. Feed back and compare answers.

Read about it

1 Students discuss the pre reading questions in pairs. Feed back and compare answers.

2 Set reading task as individual work and pair check.

> **Key**
> 1 d   2 b   3 d   4 c   5 a   6 c

Talk about it

Read through the useful phrases and set discussion as pair work or group work.

Feed back and compare ideas.

Write about it

Set writing task in class or for homework.

Extra activities

1 Students find collocations for these words in the text.

> curiosity   idea   coincidence   simple   information
> majority   awareness

Key

idle curiosity   **faintest** idea (for negatives)
pure coincidence   **perfectly** simple   **vital** information
great majority   **acute** awareness

2 Write these words and phrases on the board. Ask students to find words or phrases in the article with the same meaning. This could be a timed activity or a competition to see which student is able to find the answers first.

> **1** pretends something is not happening
> **2** was the first to do something
> **3** with his/her eyes covered
> **4** hunters
> **5** being followed without their knowledge
> **6** happen partly at the same time
> **7** groups of birds
> **8** win easily
> **9** massive movement of snow
> **10** cause something to happen

Key

1 ignore   2 pioneered   3 blindfolded   4 predators
5 stalked   6 overlap   7 flocks   8 beat us hands down
9 avalanche   10 set off

3 Conduct the 'staring' experiment in class. Does it work?

Life in the fast lane

Summary

Topic: speed; traffic problems

Vocabulary: collocations; language for writing a survey report

Main task: writing a letter using different sources

Subsidiary tasks: discussion; giving opinions

Warmer

Ask students if they enjoy going at high speeds.

Elicit examples of the fastest speeds they have travelled at, when this was and descriptions of how they felt.

Procedure

Lead in
Students discuss the questions in pairs. Feed back and compare answers.

Word work
1 Students complete the matching task individually and then check answers with a partner before checking as a class.

Key

impose fines/penalties   flout the speed limit
break the speed limit   drive recklessly
enforce the speed limit   speed cameras
ignore the speed limit   lower the speed limit
put your foot on the gas   be inconsiderate to road users

---

2 Explain meanings and give contexts as necessary.

Students practise the collocations individually and in pairs.

Feed back and compare sentences.

Write about it
1 Students read about the problem and discuss questions in pairs.

2 Read through the suggested solutions and quotes and check meanings.

3 Refer students to the words in the box and instruct them to complete the gapped phrases. Check answers as a class.

Key

1 shows   **2** according   **3** clear   **4** people   **5** number
6 major

---

2 Discuss the writing task and go through what should be included in the letter. Students write the letter. Monitor and give advice.

Talk about it
Students discuss the quotations in pairs. Feed back and compare ideas as a class.

Extra activity
1 Students role play the council meeting to discuss the points raised in the letters they have received. This can be done either as pairwork or in small groups. They can be given these roles.

> a councillor who cares more about money than people's safety
>
> a councillor who cares more about people's safety than money
>
> a councillor who is practical and realistic

2 Students write a letter from the council in reply to the residents' letter.

Dress to impress

Summary

Topic: image; fashion; dress codes

Vocabulary: word building: opposites; collocations

Main task: discussion

Subsidiary tasks: writing a letter of complaint

Warmer

Ask students to close their eyes and describe to their partner what you (or their partner) are/is wearing.

Procedure

Lead in

Students discuss questions in pairs. Feed back and compare answers.

Word work

Students answer the questions in pairs. Feed back and ask students to write/give sentences to show how the adjectives are used.

Key

1 informal   inappropriate   unsuitable   unacceptable
inoffensive   disrespectful
2 formality   appropriacy/appropriateness   suitability
acceptance   offence   respect

Talk about it

1 Students answer the questions in pairs and then compare answers as a class.

Elicit other occasions when a dress code operates.

2 Set matching task as pair work. Feed back and ask if students think these are reasonable requests. There may be some discussion about the answers.

Key

1 beach   **2** shopping   **3** night club   **4** wedding
5 a party

3 a Students match collocations individually and then check in pairs. Feedback.

Key

1 e   **2** d   **3** a   **4** c   **5** b

b Students discuss the question in pairs or small groups. If necessary, give personal example. Feed back and compare ideas.

4 Read through list of expressions and check students understand meanings.

Repeat expressions with students for pronunciation practice.

Students read about the situations and then discuss in pairs.

Feed back ideas for discussion.

Write about it

Revise/Elicit what should be included in letter of complaint. Set task in class or for homework.

Extra activity

1 a Put students into pairs and ask them to use a dictionary to make other words from these words from the unit.

> expose   dismiss   naturist   impress   celebration
> compulsory

b Ask the pairs to write gapped sentences with the words they have made and to exchange these with other pairs.

2 Ask students to bring in (or provide) news items where people have acted or reacted in certain ways to situations concerning image. Alternatively, ask them to imagine situations and make a note of them and hand them in.

Put students into pairs and supply them with one of the news items or ideas. Ask them to create a short dialogue agreeing/disagreeing with the behaviour to practise using the expressions on page 13 of the Student's Book.

It's good to **gossip**

Summary

Topic: gossip; rumours

Vocabulary: verbs and expressions related to gossip

Main task: listening to a radio interview for gist and specific information

Subsidiary tasks: discussion; writing a dialogue

Warmer

Say *Did you know…?* with exaggerated intonation and elicit what might follow to establish concept of gossiping/rumours.

Put students into pairs and ask them to tell each other a rumour (real or imagined) and then feed back the rumours to the class.

Procedure

Lead in

Students discuss questions in pairs. Feed back and compare answers.

Word work

1 Set task as individual work and ask students to check in pairs. Feed back and elicit more examples of people doing these things.

Key

1 sweet talk   2 whinge/moan about/go off on one
3 diss   4 go on and on   5 make small talk   6 flatter

2 🔘 **6.1** Students predict where the stress will be. Play the recording for them to check and practise.

Key

1 I'll do **all** your laundry for a **month** if you say yes!
2 The film was **rubbish**, the coffee was **cold** and it was **freezing** in the cinema.
3 He has **no tact** at **all** when he's talking to people.
4 I cannot **believe** he did that to you. Wait till I see him! My brother is the **biggest cheater** on this planet and I'm **sick** of him thinking he can just treat every girl he goes out with so badly. You wait till I tell **Mum** about this latest …
5 Weather's **brilliant** again, isn't it? What did you get up to **yesterday** then?
6 You're about the most **intelligent** guy I've met in **years**. A **first** from Cambridge – that's **amazing**. Tell me about your **research** in that lovely **Ferrari** of yours.

3 Set task as pair work. Monitor and choose students to give examples to class.

4 Set matching task as individual work and get students to check answers in pairs.

Key

1 spreading rumours
2 A rumour's going round
3 to keep it to yourself
4 it's not public knowledge
5 keep your ear to the ground
6 behind his back

Listen

1 🔘 **6.2** Discuss the question with students and play the recording to check their ideas.

2 🔘 **6.2** Students listen to the recording again to complete the true/false task. Check answers as a class and explain any unknown vocabulary.

Key

1 F   **2** F   **3** T   **4** F   **5** T   **6** F

3 🔘 **6.2** Students listen to choose correct alternatives. Check. Discuss ideas raised in the listening in full group or pairs.

Read through the phrases with the students. Elicit which were used in the dialogue. Students listen to check. Practise pronunciation with students. Students practise reading the dialogue (from the tapescript) in pairs.

Key

1 five   **2** social   **3** feel-   **4** natural   **5** deny

Write about it

Set task as pair work. If there is time, students can write the dialogues in class, otherwise they can complete them for homework.

Extra activity

This can be done before or after the task in Write about it.

Put students into pairs, A and B, and arrange the pairs in a rough circle.

Ask each pair to invent a rumour (as complex as they can make them).

Student A passes this on the student on the left. Student B turns to student on his/her right to be told another rumour which he/she then passes on to Student A, and so on. Rumours circulate.

After all rumours have been passed round the class, ask for final students receiving the rumours to relate them to the class. Have they changed in any way?

Born or made?

Summary

Topic: entrepreneurs; personal qualities

Vocabulary: personality adjectives; sayings

Main task: reading an article for detailed understanding

Subsidiary tasks: discussion of related issues; writing a short article

Warmer

Before students open their books write *REPTERRTNUNEE* on the board and ask them to rearrange the letters to make the word or play hangman to elicit it.

Procedure

Lead in

1 Students discuss questions in pairs. Feed back and compare answers.

2 Students read the sayings and compare their ideas in groups. Feed back. Do they know of any similar sayings from their own countries?

Word work

1 Set task as pair work. Check that students can give correct definitions or examples.

2 Students complete the task individually and then discuss in pairs. Feed back and compare examples.

Read about it

1 Students answer the questions in pairs.

2 Students read to check answers.

Key

1 Bill Gates   Richard Branson   Philip Green
2 £5 million   3 fifty percent   4 Bill Gates

3 Students answer the questions individually and then check answers in pairs.

Key

1 They are important for the economy.
2 twins – because they have same genes.
3 meeting the right people, winning money, having opportunities
4 They aren't very successful in higher education.

4 + 5 Set vocabulary tasks as pair work. Check and explain further unfamiliar lexis.

Key

1 sideline
2 following in the footsteps of
3 vital
4 it goes without saying
5 encounters
6 play its part
7 dropped out

Talk about it

Set discussion task as pair work and feed back to full group discussion.

Write about it

Set writing task in class or for homework as appropriate.

Extra activities

1 To practise adjectives, ask students to look at the words for 1 minute and then test their spelling. Alternatively, they can test each other in pairs.

2 Before the writing activity, choose an entrepreneur famous in the students' country (or worldwide) and play 'Who am I? 20 questions'. Students can then do the same in pairs as a lead in to the writing task.

Have your say

Summary

Topic: influencing change; protesting

Vocabulary: collocations, expressions for giving opinions

Main task: writing a comment for a website

Subsidiary tasks: discussion of related issues; pronunciation practice

Warmer

Write *Referendum* on board. Elicit examples of what issues can be addressed by referendums.

Ask students how important referendums are and whether, once elected, politicians should be left to make the decisions.

Procedure

Lead in

Students discuss questions in pairs. Feed back and compare ideas.

Word work

1 Students do matching task in pairs.

Discuss question in full group and ask for examples of when students have/would do these things and why.

Tell students to cover lists. Test collocations by giving first part and eliciting the second.

Key

1 d **2** e **3** a **4** g **5** h **6** b **7** c **8** f

2 a Students complete sentences individually and check in pairs.

b 🔘 **8.1** Students listen to check their answers.

Key

1 make **2** point **3** silent **4** leave **5** along
6 bother, pointless **7** done **8** less **9** apathetic
10 cares **11** bit **12** feelings

3 🔘 **8.1** Read the comments aloud for students to repeat. Check stressed words.

Elicit whether statements show the speaker is concerned (C) or unconcerned (U). Listen to check. Discuss the attitudes shown.

Key

1 U **2** U **3** C **4** U **5** U **6** U **7** C **8** U **9** C
10 U **11** C **12** C

Write about it

1 Explain idea of website where people can express their opinions on different topics. Ask students whether they have ever contributed to such sites and what they think of them.

Read through the Useful language with students. Check pronunciation and elicit contexts for each phrase.

Set writing task. Emphasise that as in a chatroom there is to be **no** speaking. Check understanding of topics.

After activity, elicit some summaries of the conversations.

2 Set comment writing task for class or homework.

Talk about it

Discuss questions as a class or in groups.

Extra activities

1 Write each of the six topics at the top of a separate blank sheet of paper. Photocopy these so that there are enough sheets to supply the class divided into groups of six.

Give each group a set of topics. Students circulate sheets within their groups, writing a comment on each.

When all students have commented on each sheet, get them to swap sheets with other groups to edit them.

2 In groups students choose a cause and write the slogan for a banner or placard.

Mind your language

Summary

Topic: language learning

Vocabulary: collocations; expressions for describing advantages and disadvantages

Main task: evaluating and ranking different courses

Subsidiary tasks: discussion of related issues; scanning adverts; writing an advert

Warmer

Greet students in another language.

Elicit in how many languages they can use to greet each other.

Ask whether any students are bilingual or have other languages they can use well. Discuss how important it is to have a second language.

Procedure

Lead in

1 a Students read the questionnaire and add their questions.

b Students complete and exchange the questionnaires. Feed back and compare answers.

2 a Students discuss comments in small groups. Feed back. Discuss why some students have these opinions.

b Elicit their own comments about language learning and discuss how many people agree.

Elicit different ways we can learn a language (types of courses).

Word work

1 Tell students the collocations are taken from adverts for language courses. Students match collocations in pairs. Check.

Key
1 d **2** g **3** k **4** a **5** i **6** l **7** c **8** f **9** b **10** h
11 j **12** e

2 Discuss the question as a class.

Read about it

1 Set reading task as individual work and put students into pairs to check. Feedback.

Key
1 E **2** C **3** A **4** F **5** B **6** G **7** D

2 Explain task and read through Useful language. Give or elicit contexts for each expression.

Students complete the task in pairs. Monitor and bring opinions into full group discussion.

Write about it

Set writing task for class or homework.

Extra activity

1 Before writing the advert, put students into small groups to discuss their ideal language course and ask them to make notes about different points.

The class then becomes a symposium for representatives to give mini presentations on their language courses. They must deal with questions from the floor.

2 Students choose one of the adverts from the reading and write a fuller advert including more details on what the course offers.

Smile please

Summary

Topic: feelings; faking emotions; attitudes to work

Vocabulary: expressions for showing emotion; expressions for cheering up

Main task: listening for gist and specific information; comparing degrees of formality

Subsidiary tasks: discussion of related issues; role play; pronunciation work; writing a summary

Warmer

Smile at the class and elicit reactions/or tell a joke and see how many students laugh or smile.

Ask what makes them smile or laugh. Put them into pairs and ask them to tell their partner something funny and report back whether he/she smiled/laughed/remained impassive or 'faked' a smile.

Can they tell when someone is faking it and do they ever fake a smile themselves? Why?

Procedure

Lead in

Students discuss questions in pairs. Feedback and compare answers.

Word work

1 Set task as pair work. Check answers. See key below.

2 Set task as pair work. Check answers. Ask students if they can identify any famous people with the expressions.

Key

he's an old misery guts (2)   she's a right whinger (2)
her smile lights up her face (1)   put a brave face on it (3)
grin and bear it (3)   keep a stiff upper lip (3)
he's always so grumpy (2)   she moans all the time (2)
he has this cheesy grin (4)   it's such a fixed smile (4)
she's really gloomy (2)   he's got such a long face (2)

Talk about it

1 a Elicit the idea of 'cheering up'. Students practice the expressions.

b 🔊 **10.1** Students listen and repeat the expressions.

2 Set role play task as pair work. Monitor and, if appropriate, ask some pairs to repeat their role plays.

Listen

1 Discuss meaning of the phrases with the class.

2 🔊 **10.2** Set listening task as individual work. Play the recording twice. Check answers.

Key

1 be herself   **2** really lost her   **3** pretend
4 ticked her off   **5** takes it out

3 🔊 **10.3** Students practise intonation by repeating the responses.

4 Elicit students' opinions on 'emotional labour'.

5 🔊 **10.4** Set listening task as individual work. Play the recording and check answers.

Key

1 professional
2 an interviewer and an expert on a radio or TV show
3 the language is much less colloquial

6 🔊 **10.4** Play the recording again for students to answer True/False questions.

Key

1 T   **2** F   **3** T   **4** F   **5** T

Talk about it

🔊 **10.4** Set speaking task. Play the recording again for students to take notes.

Students complete task in pairs. Feed back and compare ideas.

Write about it

Set slogan writing task for classwork and e-mail for homework.

Extra activity

Ask students to close their books. Write one word from each of the expressions from Word work on the board and elicit full expressions.

Something must be done

Summary

Topic: animals; complaining

Vocabulary: animal noises; expressions for complaining

Main task: reading an article for gist and specific information

Subsidiary tasks: discussion; role play; writing a letter of complaint

Warmer

Write *peacock* on the board and elicit what students know about peacocks. What adjective is associated with them? (*proud*)

Elicit other qualities associated with animals, e.g. *loyalty – dog*, etc.

Procedure

Read about it

1 a Elicit suggestions for the connection.

b Students scan the article to check. Feed back.

Key
The peacock is in love with the petrol pump.

2 Students read the article more carefully to answer questions. Check answers. Elicit any funny animal stories the students know.

Key
1 T **2** T **3** F **4** F **5** F

Word work

1 Set task as pair work. Check answers.

Key
1 dodge **2** resplendent **3** plumage **4** in the vicinity
5 screeching **6** may well be numbered

2 Set task as pair work. Compare answers as a class.

Key
1 mating **2** struck **3** bug **4** taken **5** attached

3 a + b Set task as pair work. Feed back and compare answers. Elicit how the verbs might be used to describe human activity.

Key
sound: roar (lion) bark (dog) screech (owl) yelp (dog) growl (dog) purr (cat) squeak (mouse) hiss (snake)
movement: strut (peacock) pounce (cat) trot (horse) hover (bird of prey) soar (bird)

4 Students complete the sentences individually and check in pairs.

Key
1 hovering **2** pounced **3** struts **4** plummeted
5 purred **6** barked

Talk about it

1 Set discussion question as pair work. Feed back briefly.

2 Elicit any expressions that could be used to complain in this situation.

Refer students to lists of phrases for Residents and Councillors.

Model expressions for students to practise pronunciation.

Set role play activity and students complete in pairs. Monitor and feed back.

3 Elicit what makes the Resident's expressions informal and the Councillor's more formal.

Refer students to the Useful language and ask them to match them to the informal expressions for the Residents.

Key
Possible answers
I have contacted you on many occasions.
We would like some action to be taken.
Our lives are becoming unbearable.
Be assured that we shall continue to pursue this matter.
Your company needs to take the matter seriously.
Is there no action that you can take?
What steps are you going to take?
This is unacceptable.
If you were in our situation …
I am not alone in thinking …

Write about it

Set writing task for class or homework.

Extra activity

1 If appropriate put students in pairs and get them to mime or mimic the verbs in Exercise 3. Their partner must guess the verb and then make a sentence using it.

2 Ask students to imagine what happened to the peacock and write a short follow up article for the paper.

Great British food

Summary

Topic: food, restaurants

Vocabulary: food; language for reviews and adverts

Main task: writing an advert and review

Subsidiary tasks: discussion; reading a review for lexical work

Warmer

List the ingredients of a common meal and see which student is first to guess the name. Put students into pairs to do the same.

Find out how many countries students can name a dish from.

Procedure

Lead in

1 Students discuss the questions in pairs. Feed back.

2 Set matching task as pair work. Check answers. Elicit opinions.

Key
1 bangers and mash   2 Yorksire pudding   3 spotted dick
4 star gazy pie

Read about it

1 Students read the advert to answer question. Feed back. Ask whether it sounds a good place to go.

Key
1 2

2 Elicit meaning of *expectations*. Set sentence completion task as individual work. Put students into pairs to check. Feed back.

Key
1 low   2 high, comes   3 meet, surpass   4 fell short

3 Tell students they are going to read a review of the restaurant and ask for predictions of what might be in the review. Students scan the review to check their predictions. Feed back.

Set reading task as individual work. Students compare answers in pairs.

Key
1 invited   2 admit   3 apprehension   4 visions
5 mistaken   6 back   7 treated   8 experience
9 dressed   10 education   11 die   12 accompanied
13 complemented   14 recommend   15 hype

4 Students work in pairs to find collocations. Check. Students test each other in pairs.

Key
1 puddings   2 vegetables   3 pies   4 puddings
5 meats and fish   6 experience   7 game   8 vegetables

5 Students work in pairs or small groups to find useful phrases for a review. Compare ideas as a class.

Write about it

1 Students create adverts in pairs.

2 Students exchange adverts and discuss with their partner what to include in the review. They write the reviews individually. If appropriate, they can swap reviews for editing.

Extra activity

Before writing the review students use the notes to give a presentation of their restaurant to the rest of the group/or class. Students vote on which sounds the most impressive.

Get your priorities right

Summary

Topic: prioritising; the news

Vocabulary: word building; expressions for emphasis

Main task: discussing news reporting

Subsidiary tasks: comparing priorities; organising a news report; writing a news report

Warmer

List things you have to do at the weekend and elicit *prioritise*. Establish what *top priority* means. Ask students to do the same.

Procedure

Lead in

1 Students read the comments and compare ideas.

2 Students do the task in pairs. Feed back and compare ideas.

Students discuss the questions in pairs. Feed back and compare ideas.

Word work

1 **a + b** Set task as pair work. Compare answers.

Key
Possible answers
priority/prior   choice/choosy/chosen   selection/selective
option/optional   ranked/ranking   ordered/orderly

2 Set task as individual work and put students into pairs to compare answers before checking as a class.

Key
1 choice/option   2 order   3 ranked   4 opt   5 priority
6 selection   7 rankings   8 priority   9 choosy

Talk about it

1 + 2 Set task for individual work followed by comparison and discussion in pairs. Feed back.

Listen

13.1 Play recording twice. Students compare answers in pairs before checking as a class.

Key
1 David Beckham and the Middle East
2 no
3 a footballer
4 Because she thinks the priorities are wrong.

Talk about it

1 Model the phrases for students to practise intonation. Elicit alternative endings or follow-up sentences.

Set discussion task as pair work. Feed back.

2 Students discuss headlines in pairs and put them in order of priority. Feed back and ask for reasons.

Write about it
Set writing task for class or homework.

Extra activities

1 Put students into small groups. Direct them to the list of situations in the first Talk about it section. Ask each student to choose one situation and talk for two minutes to the rest of the group about his/her priorities and reasoning behind their choices.

2 Have an open discussion with the group. Elicit what is important to them in life. Write the list on the board and discuss the priorities, e.g. money, health, happiness, etc.

3 Elicit current news stories and discuss the priority they have been given.

We know what you're doing

Summary

Topic: privacy

Vocabulary: word building; collocations

Main task: matching speakers with topics

Subsidiary tasks: discussion; word stress; writing a letter to a newspaper

Warmer

Ask students if they would ever read someone's diary, text message, email, etc. without their permission. Would it ever be acceptable? Why/Why not? Elicit *privacy*.

Procedure

Lead in
Students discuss questions in pairs. Feed back.

Word work
1 Set task as pair work. Check answers as a class.

Key

security   privacy   access   identification   secret/secrecy
protection   safety   proof   publicity

2 Students write gap fills for each other. Ask some students to read out their sentences and see who can supply the missing word.

3 Ask the class to supply contexts for the sentences. Elicit follow-up sentences.

Key

1 on private property
2 in a queue in a bank or post office
3 on the phone
4 in a newspaper or magazine

4 Set task as individual work. Check answers. Test by giving one part of the collocation to elicit the second.

Key

1 catch   **2** trace/track   **3** bug   **4** catch/tail   **5** put
6 invade/respect   **7** match   **8** steal

Listen

1 **a + b** Students complete pre listening tasks in pairs. Feed back.

2 🔘 **14.1** Explain task. Play the recording twice for students to match speakers with the topics. Check answers.

Key

A satellite navigation tracking   **B** CCTV   **C** identity cards
D DNA test   **E** phone tapping

3 a 🔘 **14.1** See if students can remember enough to do this task from memory. If not, play the recording again and check answers.

Key

1 C   **2** A   **3** E   **4** A   **5** E   **6** D   **7** C   **8** E

b Students work in pairs to think of alternative expressions. Compare ideas as a class.

4 🔘 **14.2** First ask students to work in pairs to indicate which words they think are stressed. Play the recording for students to check and then practise.

Talk about it
Put students into small groups to discuss questions. Feed back and compare ideas.

Write about it
Set writing task for class or homework.

Extra activities

1 Ask students to work in pairs to imagine how privacy laws might change over the next fifty years. Ask them to think about these things.

> What will/won't governments be able to know about us?
>
> Can we stop this or would it be a good thing/ necessary?

2 Students write a description of an occasion when they invaded someone else's privacy. They read the description to the group who have to decide if they are telling the truth or not.

They're out to get us

Summary

Topic: advertising; technology

Vocabulary: formal and informal language

Main task: reading and comparing styles of texts

Subsidiary tasks: discussion; writing a comment

Warmer

Write a popular advertising slogan on the board or sing the jingle from one. Elicit the product being advertised. Ask for further suggestions from the students.

If appropriate, put students into pairs to test each other on slogans and jingles. Feed back and ask for the students' favourite adverts.

Procedure

Lead in

Students discuss questions in pairs. Feed back.

Read about it

1 Students should look at the texts, not read them, in order to make predictions. Elicit suggestions from the class.

2 **a + b** Students look at words in pairs. Feed back. Give or elicit possible context if necessary.

3 Set reading task for pairs. After reading their texts, students ask each other questions. Feed back and check answers.

Key

Text A: graft   weirder   a snippet   hi-tech   grab   dangle

Text B: vying for   inundated   subjected to   captive audience   fine-tuned   exempt

---

4 **a + b** Students work in pairs to try to remember contexts, find and underline words. Check with the class.

5 Students read other text and discuss differences in formality in pairs. Make sure they understand that text A is less formal. Refer back to the words underlined to illustrate this if necessary.

Talk about it

Students discuss questions in pairs. Compare ideas as a class.

Write about it

Set task for class or homework.

Extra activities

1 In small groups students describe a famous advert from TV, cinema or magazine. The group must guess the product.

2 Students test each other on the new vocabulary by giving definitions to elicit the words.

3 In small groups students choose a new product and plan an advertising campaign.

For your **reference**

Summary

Topic: qualities and managerial skills

Vocabulary: word building; synonyms

Main task: writing a reference

Subsidiary tasks: discussion; reading for detailed understanding

Warmer

Write *referee* on the board and elicit different meanings.

Ask what words can be made from this (*refer/reference/referral*) and ask for contexts.

Procedure

Lead in

1 a + b Students complete questionnaire individually and then compare answers. Feed back.

2 Ask students about origin of questionnaire. If any students have completed one in the past, ask them what they think of this type of questionnaire. Do they think they are useful for employers?

Word work

1 a Students work on word work tasks in pairs. Check answers.

Key
Possible answers
reliable/reliant   judgemental   supportive   decisive
committed   trusting/trustworthy   organised
motivated/motivating   constructive   inventive
competitive   innovative   enthusiastic   professional
accessible   sensible/sensitive   personable

b Monitor students as they supply definitions for the adjectives.

2 Students complete sentences individually. Check answers with the class.

Key
1 constructive   **2** professional   **3** personable
4 committed

Talk about it

Students discuss questions in pairs. Feed back and compare ideas.

Read about it

1 Set reading task as individual work. Check answers with the class.

Ensure that they understand that the writer is trying to convey that May Thompson is an unsatisfactory employee.

2 Students complete task individually and compare answers in pairs.

Key
1 worked for
2 in her time with us
3 started work here
4 the tasks she is employed to do
5 adequate
6 regarding
7 innovative
8 attributes this to the fact that

Write about it

Students can prepare writing task in pairs if appropriate.

Set writing task for individual work. Students exchange references for editing.

Extra activities

1 In small groups students choose a job and write down the qualities and skills a person might need for this job. They then read their list to the class. Other students must guess what job they are talking about.

2 Divide class into groups and give a quiz on new words. E.g. *Give the noun form of the word 'construct'.*

3 Set up a role play where students ask and answer questions about a third party on the phone. First in pairs students write a role play card about an imaginary employee with the 'real' (and unappealing) facts. E.g. *He always eats crisps at his desk.* They exchange cards with another pair. They then have to give a phone reference about the person on the card, trying not to say anything directly bad about him/her.

Making **money**

Summary

Topic: starting a business

Vocabulary: collocations

Main task: role play of potential businesses and investors

Subsidiary tasks: discussion; listening for information and expressions; practising intonation

Warmer

Ask students who is the richest person they know and how he/she made their money. Elicit possible good and bad qualities of a multi millionaire.

Procedure

Lead in

Students discuss questions in pairs. Feed back and compare ideas.

Word work

1 Students match words to make collocations individually and check answers in pairs Feedback. Elicit contexts if necessary.

Key

1 g **2** f **3** e **4** i **5** a/c/g **6** a **7** b **8** d **9** h

2 Students replace words in italics individually. Check answers with the class.

Key

1 sound investment **2** initial outlay **3** break even
4 find a backer

3 Ask students to write two more sentences each like this.

Students test each other in pairs.

Listen

1 [🔊] **17.1** Play the recording once. Ask students to make a note of the answers and check as a class.

Key

1 niece and uncle **2** beauty salon **3** he might

2 [🔊] **17.1** Read through the expressions with students. Set task as pair work. Play the recording again for students to check.

Key

1 good head for business **2** past me **3** through
4 costs **5** talk

Talk about it

1 Students discuss the questions in pairs.

2 Explain the role play. Model expressions for students to copy and check meanings.

3 Set task for rotating role play. Give students preparation time. If possible, arrange a circle of desks with pairs of business partners on the outside and pairs of potential investors on the inside facing them.

Monitor role play and allow each conversation an appropriate time (e.g. five minutes) before saying *Time's up/Move on/All change*, etc. At this point investors stand up and move to their right to sit opposite another pair of partners.

Finish by asking investors which businesses they would invest in and why.

Extra activity

Students write a follow up letter after the role play. Investors write a formal offer and give reasons why they like the proposal. Business partners write a letter to potential investors reminding them of their proposals and attempting to persuade them to invest.

Wired for sound

Summary

Topic: music; background music; noise

Vocabulary: expressions for giving opinions

Main task: listening to a conversation for detailed information

Subsidiary tasks: discussion; practising intonation; writing a dialogue

Warmer

Ask students about most recent music downloads and CDs they have bought. Which artist is class favourite, which artists do class predict will be most successful in the coming months?

Procedure

Lead in

1 Students discuss questions in pairs. Feed back.

2 a Refer students to pictures and set task for pair work. Feed back.

b 🔘 **18.1** Play the recording. Students compare the reasons given against having background music with their own ideas.

Listen

1 🔘 **18.1** Play the recording again and tell students to tick the pictures mentioned and note any other places that are discussed.

Key
Pictures mentioned:
2 (a designer clothes shop) **3** (a restaurant)
5 (a supermarket) **6** (holding on the phone)
Other places mentioned: chemists, train, hospital, tube

2 Students complete the matching task individually and check in pairs.

Key
1 b **2** d **3** e **4** c **5** a

3 🔘 **18.1** Read through phrases and elicit whether students can remember who said them. Play the recording again for students to check.

Key
1 L **2** L **3** S **4** S **5** L **6** L **7** S **8** L **9** L **10** L
11 L **12** S

4 a Set task as individual work.

b 🔘 **18.2** Play the recording to check answers. Elicit other possible endings from the class.

Key
1 c **2** d **3** f **4** e **5** a **6** b

5 a 🔘 **18.3** Ask two students to read the dialogue aloud. Ask students in pairs to predict where the stress patterns are. Play the recording for students to check.

b Students practise reading the dialogue in pairs.

Talk about it

Ask what a street musician is and elicit different types.

Students discuss the statement in pairs or small groups. Feed back.

Write about it

Set writing task as pair work in class or individual work at home.

Extra activity

Put students into small groups. Write a list of related topics on the board.

- Why I prefer working in silence/with background music
- My parents' taste in music
- How my musical tastes have changed
- I prefer live/recorded music
- The future of CDs
- The best and worst CDs I have ever bought

Students choose a topic and talk about it for two minutes without stopping.

The hands of time

Summary

Topic: image; cosmetic surgery

Vocabulary: words with similar meanings; expressions for survey findings

Main task: multiple choice cloze; reading for detailed information

Subsidiary tasks: discussion; writing a summary of survey results

Warmer

On the board write names of a film star famous for his/her looks, a rap artist and a top fashion model and elicit what students associate with these people.

Procedure

Lead in

Students discuss questions in pairs. Feed back.

Word work

1 Students work on the words individually and compare answers in pairs. Monitor and feed back as necessary.

2 Students complete the sentences and check answers in pairs.

Elicit further examples of sentences using some of the words in context.

Key

1 appearance   2 smart   3 scruffy   4 classy

Read about it

1 Set task as pair work. Feed back.

2 Give students a short time to scan the text to check answers.

Key

All procedures are mentioned except tattoo removals.

3 Set task as individual work and put students into pairs to check answers. Explain meanings of any unfamiliar words.

Key

1 c   2 b   3 b   4 a   5 c   6 c   7 a   8 b   9 b
10 a   11 a

4 Students complete task individually. Check answers with the class.

Key

nine – nine million cosmetic procedures
40 – 40% rise in demand for some procedures by older women
22 – 22% increase in procedures last year

Talk about it

1 **a + b** Set task as pair work. Students exchange ideas and note down other students' opinions.

Write about it

Set writing task for class or homework.

Extra activity

Ask students to work in pairs to write an advertisement for a private cosmetic clinic. They should think about these things.

- range of procedures
- cost
- accommodation

They can then present their clinic to the rest of the class. The class votes on the most popular clinic.

Our survey says

Summary

Topic: surveys; holidays; stress at work

Vocabulary: phrases in surveys

Main task: writing a report using given information

Subsidiary tasks: discussion

Warmer

Conduct a brief class survey to establish concept. Ask how many students came to school **a** on foot **b** by car **c** by bus **d** any other way. Write the results on the board and elicit *survey*. Establish *over half*, *a quarter*, etc., and ask why people conduct surveys like this.

Procedure

Lead in

Students discuss questions in pairs. Feed back. Do students find surveys annoying or are they happy to provide the information asked for?

Read about it

1 Students ask and answer the survey questions in pairs. Compare answers with the class.

2 Set the task as pair work.

3 Students scan the survey to check answers.

Key

1 a South Korea **b** 2,317 **2 a** France **b** 1,481
3 a Brazil **b** 30 **4 a** Hong Kong **b** 9

Word work

Set task as individual work. Check that students are using the phrases correctly. Write up good examples on the board.

Talk about it

Students discuss the questions in pairs. Compare answers with the class.

Write about it

1 **a** Discuss commuting and stress in pairs, then compare ideas with the class.

b Students read survey results. Ask whether any of the results are surprising.

2 Read through the list of useful phrases and set writing task for individual work and pair editing.

Extra activities

1 In small groups students design a class survey about some aspect of stress. They should think of a topic and write the questions. They circulate to ask and answer questions and then compile results. They can write a report for homework or give an oral report to the other groups.

If they have problems thinking of topics for the survey, brainstorm ideas before they start work. Example topics: stress in the workplace, exam stress for students, fast pace of life today, etc.

2 Test students' memory of phrases. Ask them to close their books. Write key words on the board to elicit phrases. E.g. *comment*, *based*, *vast*, *among*, etc.

All change

Summary

Topic: change in appearance/personality; life changing events

Vocabulary: idioms

Main task: giving a short talk

Subsidiary tasks: discussion; listening for gist and detailed information; writing an e-mail

Warmer

If possible bring in two photos of a famous person – one current, one taken some time ago. Alternatively, write the name of a famous person (film star/presenter/sportsman/ politician) on the board with two dates that students will associate with them (e.g. the year film star made most famous film and the date today). Elicit how the person has changed between the two dates/photos. Focus on lifestyle and personality as well as appearance.

Procedure

Lead in

1 Students discuss questions in pairs. Compare answers with the class.

2 Set role play task. Ask students to imagine themselves in a situation e.g. they go to a school reunion, they are both waiting for an interview for a job, etc. Monitor role plays.

3 Ask students to tell class how they have changed.

Listen

1 🔘 **21.1** Set task as individual work. Play the recording. Check answers.

Key
1 G   2 B   3 B   4 G   5 B

2 🔘 **21.1** Set task as individual work and play the recording again. Ask students to compare answers in pairs before checking with the class.

Key
Beth mentions university (uni) and Gemma mentions splitting up with her boyfriend.

3 Students work in pairs to match the phrases. Check answers and establish the difference in levels of formality. Model phrases for pronunciation work.

Key
1 d   2 h   3 g   4 e   5 b   6 f   7 i   8 a   9 c

4 🔘 **21.1** Students practise reading the dialogue in pairs.

Talk about it

1 Students discuss meanings and contexts for the sayings in pairs or small groups.

2 **a** Students prepare to give short talks on one of the topics. Check through expressions in box.

b Students give talks in small groups. Feed back any interesting comments.

Write about it

Set writing task for class or homework.

Extra activities

1 Students choose a pair of famous people and repeat the role play from Lead in Exercise 2 (e.g. Brad Pitt and Jennifer Anniston meet up five years after they split).

2 Students write the dialogue from either of the role plays.

Time on your side

Summary

Topic: time; punctuality

Vocabulary: expressions with *time*; colloquial expressions

Main task: listening to an anecdote for general and detailed information

Subsidiary tasks: discussion, telling an anecdote, writing an anecdote

Warmer

Ask the class what the time is to see how many students have watches, look at mobile phones, etc. Elicit where we can find out what the time is (alarm clocks, clocks in public buildings, in classrooms, speaking clock, etc.). Could students live without a watch?

Procedure

Lead in

1 Students discuss questions in pairs. Compare ideas with the class.

2 Students discuss meanings of quotes in small pairs. Compare ideas with the class.

Word work

1 Elicit expressions using the word *time* and write them on the board. Refer students to the task and check how many are the same. Students work in pairs to add any more expressions. Feed back.

Key
Additional expressions
It's about time!   waste time   beat time

2 Set task as individual work and check.

Key
1 I've told you time after time …
2 I think she's on borrowed time since …
3 There's a time limit of an hour for this work.
4 We had the time of our lives …
5 I'm sorry, you're out of time.

Listen

1 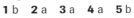 Elicit the meaning *anecdote*. Set task and play the recording. Check answers.

Key
1 informal
2 *Home at last* because it suggests the sense of relief after a stressful journey when lots of different things happened.

2 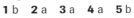 Play the recording again. Students complete the task individually then check in pairs.

Key
1 b   2 a   3 a   4 a   5 b

3 Students work in pairs to find formal equivalents. Check.

Key
Suggested answers
1 Ordinarily
2 quite difficult regarding timing
3 made my contribution, this is the complete truth
4 ran
5 got on, We were so lucky!
6 very hungry
7 thought/imagined, sleep
8 manage to travel, there was a slight chance
9 ran
10 In retrospect

4 Put students into pairs to write their sentences. If possible, swap the sentences around the class for completion.

Talk about it

Give students time to prepare an anecdote. This can be true or imagined. Run through sequencing words. Students tell their anecdote in pairs or small groups. Invite some students to tell their stories to the class.

Write about it

Set writing task for class or homework.

Extra activity

Students rewrite the anecdote in a more formal style as an essay.

Happiness

Summary

Topic: happiness and unhappiness

Vocabulary: adjectives to describe feelings

Main task: reading to identify main topics and for detailed information

Subsidiary tasks: discussion; writing a comment for a website

Warmer

Ask students how they are feeling. Establish that some are feeling happy and ask them to specify why. Elicit when they feel happiest and unhappiest. Has this changed over the years?

Procedure

Lead in

Students discuss questions in pairs. Compare ideas with the class.

Word work

1 **a** Students brainstorm words for *happy* and *sad* in pairs. Write up the words on the board.

b Students look at the adjectives in the box and check to see how many they have already thought of.

2 Students categorise the words according to whether they describe the normal range of feelings or extreme feelings. This is likely to cause some discussion.

Key
Suggested answers
Normal: happy, contented, sad, miserable, fed up, down
Extreme: blissful, overjoyed, ecstatic, delirious, elated, depressed, suicidal

Read about it

1 **a + b** Students discuss questions and then as a class.

2 **a** Discuss possible answers to problems with the class.

b Set task as individual work and put students in pairs to compare answers. Check answers with the class.

Key
A the media **B** materialism **C** families
D unfairness in society **E** television

3 Set task as individual work. Check.

Key
1 D, E **2** B **3** A **4** C **5** E **6** D

4 Students match words and phrases in pairs. Check answers with the class.

Key
1 sensationalist **2** vanishing **3** breeds discontentment
4 promote **5** outright **6** gawp **7** at first hand

Talk about it

Discuss the questions as a class.

Write about it

Set writing task for class or homework.

Extra activity

Ask students to write down their top ten pieces of advice on how to be happy. Give some suggested headings.

- Don't …
- Always …
- Never …

Feed back advice and compile a class top five.

File in bin
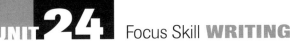

Summary

Topic: junk mail; cold calling

Vocabulary: expressions and collocations

Main task: using information to complete an article

Subsidiary tasks: discussion; reading article for gist; writing a magazine article

Warmer

Play a game of 20 questions to elicit the job of postman. What is good or bad about the job? Elicit whether students still write letters, when and who to. What post do their families receive? Write a list on the board.

Procedure

Lead in

Students discuss the questions in pairs. Compare answers with the class.

Read about it

1 Set task as individual work. Check answers with the class.

Elicit a summary sentence for the paragraph. Check students understand *round*, *distributing*, *understandably unhappy*, *in the balance*, *highlight*.

Key
1 F   **2** T   **3** F

2 Students discuss the questions. Feed back.

3 **a** Tell students that the collocations and expressions come from the second part of the article which they do not have. Students complete matching task in pairs.

b Students compare their answers and imagine possible contexts. Ask for some example sentences and write them on the board.

Key
1 e   **2** c   **3** h   **4** a   **5** g   **6** i   **7** d   **8** f   **9** j   **10** b

Write about it

1 **a + b** Set writing task. Explain that students should write the rest of the article using the information given. First put them into pairs to check the meanings of the words in italics and categorise the list of facts.

Key
Amount: 1, 2, 5, 6, 8, 10, 7
Environment: 3
Solutions: 4, 9, 12

2 Give students time to plan their articles and remind them of the suggested structure.

Students write the article. If appropriate, they can swap and edit each other's articles.

3 Students work in pairs to plan the magazine article. Students write individually in class or for homework.

Extra activity

Bring in a collection of junk mail. Give an item to each pair of students. The pairs read the junk mail and summarise the information it provides and what is being advertised. Students assess the value of their item and tell the group about it. The class can then vote on how many items have any value.

How are you?

Summary

Topic: health issues; private and state care

Vocabulary: expressing opinions

Main task: presenting, defending and opposing causes

Subsidiary tasks: discussion; work on stress; listening for gist and specific information; writing an article

Warmer

Think of a health problem and ask students where you could go or get advice on this. Write a list on the board: *hospital, doctor's surgery, magazine column, Internet, phone lines*, etc. Ask students to assess how useful they are. Are students happy with health care in their country?

Procedure

Lead in

Students discuss the questions in pairs. Compare ideas with the class.

Read about it

1 Set task as individual work and feed back. Check students understand *funded, treatment, balance its books, controversial*.

2 Students compare health systems in pairs. Compare ideas with the class.

Talk about it

1 + 2 Students read headlines individually and compare ideas in pairs. Ask some students to report back to the class.

Listen

1 🔘 **25.1** Play the recording and allow students to listen for general understanding. Ask students to complete the dialogues and play the recording again to check the answers.

Key

1 single	**2** priority	**3** pushed	**4** care	**5** miracle cure
6 pricy	**7** nose job	**8** damaging	**9** stopped	**10** up to

2 Students work in pairs to match the dialogues with the headlines.

Key

1 C **2** B **3** A **4** E **5** D

Talk about it

1 **a** Explain that students are going to have a class discussion and read through the expressions.

b 🔘 **25.2** Ask students to mark the stress. Play the recording for them to check and practise pronunciation.

2 Students prepare in pairs.

3 Students then present cause to the group and criticise or defend the other causes.

Write about it

Set writing task for class or homework.

Extra activity

On the board, write *Organ donation should be obligatory*. Check that students understand what this refers to. Ask them to write down a set of sentences related to the topic using each new expression from the unit. Feed back.

Respect

Summary

Topic: respect; behaviour

Vocabulary: words with similar meanings; expression for stating opinions

Main task: matching speakers and topics

Subsidiary tasks: discussion; ranking; writing a paragraph

Warmer

Write the anagram *PRETESC* on the board and see which student can solve it first. If they need help give the definition: *a feeling of admiration for someone/something because of their good qualities or achievements.*

Elicit collocations, e.g. *respect someone's privacy/opinions/decision*, etc. Explain that the prefix *dis-* can be used informally: *to disrespect/diss someone.*

Procedure

Lead in

Students discuss questions in pairs. Feed back and compare ideas.

Word work

Read through the words to check pronunciation. Set task as pair work. Check answers. Elicit a context for those words not used.

Key

1 respect   2 tradition   3 custom   4 manners
5 respectable   6 consideration

Listen

1 **a** Put students into groups to predict possible attitudes.

   b 🔘 **26.1** Play the recording. Students check their ideas.

2 🔘 **26.1** Play the recording again. Students listen to match opinions and speakers.

Key

1 F   2 D   3 D   4 M   5 F   6 M   7 S   8 F

3 **a** Set task as individual work and ask students to check in pairs.

   b 🔘 **26.2** Play the recording and check answers with the class. Encourage students to check the meaning of unknown words and elicit examples.

Key

1 b   2 c   3 a   4 c   5 c   6 b

Talk about it

1 Set discussion and ranking as pairwork task. Read through the expressions before students complete the task.

2 Encourage students to give reasons/explanations as they compare opinions.

Write about it

Set writing task for class or homework.

Extra activity

Write *Role Models* on the board and elicit the types of people who become role models. Students prepare to talk for a minute about someone who was a role model for them and give their talks in small groups.

Reader, I married him

Summary

Topic: reading; genres

Vocabulary: descriptive language; style

Main task: reading for gist and detailed understanding

Subsidiary tasks: discussion; predicting; writing a fictional text

Warmer

Write the name of a famous writer on the board. Ask what students know about him/her and the genre he/she writes in (romance, thriller, etc.). Elicit other genres and writers (both from students' countries and other countries)

Procedure

Lead in
Students discuss questions in pairs. Feed back and check what students read for leisure as opposed to work/study.

Read about it
1 Student A reads Extract A and student B reads Extract B. After reading they ask each other questions to build up a picture of the extract they haven't read. Feed back and check answers.

Key
Extract A
1 Alex Gray
2 detective/mystery
3 Marshal Bede
4 He worked at the same school as Marshall Bede (Marhsall Bede was his boss). He hated him. He didn't kill him.
5 He is pleased and maybe a little fearful.
6 Marshall Bede, an unpopular principal of a boarding school, has been killed – not by Alex Gray.

Extract B
1 Nina
2 romance
3 a man in the check-in queue at an airport
4 She is travelling alone. She has packed a lot of things. She likes to daydream.
5 She is interested (the man seems attractive) and envious of the blonde girl who is with him.
6 Nina has seen an interesting man in a queue. She has heard his voice but hasn't been able to see his face.

---

2 + 3 Students discuss the questions in pairs. Compare ideas with the class.

4 When students have read both extracts, do a class poll to see which one they preferred.

Write about it
1 Put students into pairs to prepare the writing task.

2 Students write the continuation of the story individually. When they have finished, they exchange pages for other students to read and compare. Which is closest in style to the original? Which is most interesting?

Extra activities
1 Write this list of British writers on the board.

> Charles Dickens   William Shakespeare
> Agatha Christie   Arthur Conan Doyle   J K Rowling
> C S Lewis   Virginia Woolf   Ian Fleming
> Lewis Carroll   J R Tolkein   Jane Austen

In pairs students try to name a book for each writer. Here are some suggestions:

Oliver Twist, Romeo and Juliet, Murder on the Orient Express, The Adventures of Sherlock Homes, Harry Potter and the Order of the Phoenix, The Lion, the Witch and the Wardrobe, To the Lighthouse, Casino Royale, Alice's Adventures in Wonderland, The Fellowship of the Ring, Pride and Prejudice

2 Copy out the first paragraph of an easy English Reader on the board. Students discuss what level they think it is and write the rest of the first page

What bugs you?

Summary

Topic: complaining; expressing emotion

Vocabulary: expressions for complaining; formal and informal equivalents

Main task: writing a letter of complaint

Subsidiary tasks: discussion; listening for detailed information; work on stress

Warmer

Tell the class about the last time you complained about something. Elicit examples from students.

Procedure

Lead in

1 Students complete the questionnaire and discuss with partner. Feed back.

2 Students think of more examples of situations that annoy them. Check ideas with the class and write up some examples on the board as a prompt for the next task.

3 Read through the expressions in the useful language box. Students work with a new partner to talk about different situations. Remind them to use the expressions if possible.

Word work

Set task for individual work and pair check. Explain meanings if necessary.

Key
1 R   2 R   3 N   4 N   5 N   6 R   7 N   8 N   9 R
10 N

Listen

1 [28.1] Check students understand the task and ask them to close their books before playing the recording. Students check answers in pairs.

Key
Speaker mentions: not enough trains in the rush hour; the cost; having to stand; the smell; safety; clothes; stress

2 [28.1] Students listen again and underline words that are stressed. Check answers, playing the recording again if necessary. Students practise in pairs.

Key
Stressed words:
good rant   cannot   extra on at the height   rush hour   appalling   sky-high   stand   whole journey   other   packed   really smelly   no way   drink   spilling   safest   work   back   feet   creased   smelly   frazzled   ages

3 Students complete the task in pairs Check answers with the class.

Key
every day   packed   whole   not the safest way to travel   prices   sky-high   extra   rush hour

Write about it

1 [28.2] Explain writing task. Play the recording and students note down points. Check that they are all agreed on the main points.

Key
Speaker mentions: hotel not completed; back room; view of building work; noise; couldn't stay in room; dirty beach; bad food at hotel

2 Students write letter in class. Ask them to exchange letters and check each other's work.

Extra activities

1 Students write another letter of complaint about one of the situations they have discussed at the beginning of the lesson.

2 In pairs students write a dialogue for one of the situations in the lesson.

3 Test expressions by giving one word to elicit complete expressions. E.g. *bother*, *fuss*, *lying down*, etc.

Green light

Summary

Topic: the environment

Vocabulary: expressions for giving a presentation

Main task: preparing and giving a presentation

Subsidiary tasks: discussion; writing a presentation

Warmer

Write *GREEN* on the board and elicit connotations. Ask students in pairs to write down as many 'green issues' as they can in one minute. Compare ideas with the class.

Procedure

Lead in

Students discuss questions in pairs. Compare ideas with the class.

Word work

Set task as pair work. Check answers with the class. Elicit other possible contexts for the expressions.

Key

1 a, c, e   **2** b, d, f, g

Listen

1 **29.1** Ask what a presentation is and where you might hear one. Set task as individual work. Play the recording. Check answers.

Key

1 to introduce a day of seminars   **2** e-waste
3 recycling, creative alternatives

2 Refer students to the recording script on page 93. Set task as pair work.

Key

Possible answers:

It's good to see you all here. I'd like to start by …; This morning you'll hear from a company …; … how shall we say …; I have to mention this …; … thank you very much for your attention.

3 a Read through the expressions with students and elicit possible endings for 1, 2, 4 and 5 and a follow up sentence for 3.

b **29.2** Play the recording. Students listen and repeat to practise intonation.

Talk about it

1 Students discuss questions in groups. Feed back.

2 Divide students into groups of three. Give each group a role A, B or C. Explain that they should prepare a presentation on the topic in their groups.

3 Regroup students so that there are representatives for each role. They then give their mini presentations in their groups. Students then discuss and evaluate the ideas presented.

Write about it

Set writing task for class or homework.

Extra activities

Students give mini presentations on the green issues discussed at the beginning of the lesson in small groups

Memories are made of this

Summary

Topic: memories; techniques for remembering

Vocabulary: word building

Main task: matching speakers and topics

Subsidiary tasks: discussion; listening for detailed information; giving memory tests

Warmer

Ask students if they can remember what their partner was wearing yesterday. What did they do exactly one week ago? How many details can they remember?

Procedure

Lead in

1 Read out a list of objects. These can be random. Give about ten objects. Ask students to memorise them but not to write them down.

2 Students do the quiz and in pairs compare answers.

Key

1 seven plus or minus two   2 When memories are too painful, it allows us to move on.   3 Smells activate certain brain cells which can link them with emotional responses. 4 three and a half   5 oily fish, whole grains, fruit and green vegetables   6 yes (it doesn't get worse!)   7 eight 8 70%   9 This is when we can remember exactly where we were when something traumatic/emotional happened.

3 Students write down the objects from the list read out in Exercise 1. Was anyone able to remember all the objects?

4 Tell students you are going to give them some instructions but not to do anything until you finish:

Draw a plan of a room. There is a table in the middle of the room. There are four chairs – one on each side of the table. There is a window on the top wall. There is a vase on the table. There is a chair in the top right hand corner.

Tell them they can start. Then say:

Just one moment – there are also two doors – one in the wall on the right and one in the wall at the bottom. OK continue.

The last instruction should mean they don't remember the previous ones very well because their processing time was interrupted.

Word work

Set task as pair work.

Key

remember; memory/remembrance
forget; forgetful/forgetfulness/forgettable/unforgettable
recall; recollection
remind; reminder
reminisce; reminiscence; reminiscent
memorise; memory/memorisation/memorial; memorable
nostalgia; nostalgic

Listen

1 🔘 **30.1** Play the recording. Students complete the task individually and check in pairs before class feed back.

Key

a 3   **b** 1   **c** 2   **d** 4

2 🔘 **30.1** Play the recording again. Students draw their sketches individually and compare them in pairs.

3 🔘 **30.1** Play the recording again. Students complete task individually. Compare answers with the class. Refer to the recording script on pages 93–94 if necessary.

Key

1 rabbit –toy at the end of the pram
2 a tree – dead tree in the middle of the field
3 a tennis game – couldn't remember the word net
4 black smoke – coming from a fire in the street

Talk about it

1 Students tell each other their memories in pairs. Feed back.

2 Students discuss questions in pairs or as a class.

3 Students work in pairs to match techniques. Feed back and compare answers.

Key

1 external aid   **2** chunking   **3** routine   **4** word play
5 place it   **6** cramming   **7** make it meaningful
8 imagery

4 **a + b** Students create lists and test each other.

Extra activity

Students choose one of the points from *Talk about it* Exercise 1 and write an account for a magazine.

Junk **culture**

Summary

Topic: junk culture; childhood

Vocabulary: compound adjectives

Main task: reading an article to identify topics and find synonyms

Subsidiary tasks: discussion; writing a formal letter

Warmer

Write *childhood* on the board (or elicit through an anagram or hangman). Brainstorm associations. What makes a good childhood? How is childhood presented in advertising and the media?

Procedure

Lead in
Students discuss the questions in pairs. Feed back.

Read about it
1 a Elicit predictions of content from the class. Write key ideas on the board to refer back to after students have read the article.

b Students read article to check predictions.

2 Set task as individual work and ask students to check in pairs before going through the answers.

Key

tick all except: music, debate, tattoos and piercings, bullying, exercise

3 Students find synonyms individually. Feed back.

Key

1 sinister   2 escalating   3 concerned   4 rapid
5 sedentary   6 significant   7 overly   8 cope with
9 exposed to   10 toxic

Word work
1 Set task as individual work. Check answers with the class. If necessary, explain unfamiliar vocabulary.

Key
1 first   2 real   3 fast   4 hyper   5 ever   6 test

2 Students write gap fills to test partners. Feedback.

Talk about it
Students discuss the questions in pairs or small groups. Feed back and bring into full group discussion.

Write about it
Set writing task for class or homework. Discuss format and formality for a letter sent to a newspaper.

Extra activity
In pairs students discuss and make notes to prepare to write a page from an imaginary diary of an eleven-year-old today. Suggest they think about: school, free time, homework, food, relationships, etc. Students write the diary page individually.

Talk to me

Summary

Topic: mobile phone culture

Vocabulary: colloquial expressions

Main task: writing arguments for and against

Subsidiary tasks: reading for gist and detailed information

Warmer

Elicit models of phones students use. Discuss the advantages and disadvantages of different models. Survey how many members of students' families have mobiles.

Procedure

Lead in

1 Students do quiz in pairs and discuss answers as a class.

2 Students discuss questions in pairs. Feed back.

Read about it

1 a Students read titles and predict content in pairs. Feedback.

  b Students scan texts to check predictions.

2 a Explain that students need to identify the main points in the argument in order to say whether they agree or disagree.

Key
Not mentioned: using the Internet

  b Students identify points included in texts and underline relevant phrases. Compare ideas as a class.

Word work

1 + 2 Set task as individual work and ask students to check in pairs before looking at the texts on page 67.

Key
1 in **2** on **3** up **4** out of **5** in, out **6** on **7** across **8** about
1 b **2** f **3** g **4** e **5** c **6** h **7** d **8** a

Write about it

1 Students discuss the different points. Feed back and write key ideas on the board before students begin writing.

2 Explain the task and go through the expressions in the useful language. Students plan their articles and write them in class or for homework.

Extra activities

1 Students combine their two articles to write one advantage and disadvantage essay. They should write their own titles.

2 Have a class discussion on one or all of the issues. One group must defend one aspect and another group the other. Take a final vote.

It's my age

Summary

Topic: age-related issues

Vocabulary: word building; collocations; words with similar meanings

Main task: discussion on aspects of age

Subsidiary tasks: reading text for general understanding; listening for specific information and general understanding; writing a magazine article

Warmer

Write *five years* on the board. Elicit that a person this age is a child. Write other ages and elicit other words: *baby/toddler/ adolescent/adult/middle-aged/elderly/old*. Elicit ages for people at these stages of life. Does everyone agree?

Procedure

Lead in
Students discuss questions in pairs. Feed back.

Word work

1 Students match pictures and words in pairs. Check answers with the class and discuss any disagreements.

2 Put students into pairs to complete the word building task Check answers with the class. Explain words if necessary and elicit additional contexts.

Key
Possible answers
juvenile (n/adj)
life expectancy: expectant   to expect
expected/unexpected   unexpectedly
precocious: precociousness   precocity
discrimination: discriminatory   to discriminate against
wisdom: wise   unwise   wisely/unwisely
maturity: mature   immature   to mature
ageism: ageist   age   underage   aged

3 Students complete sentences individually and check answers in pairs.

Key
1 discriminate   2 ageist   3 immature   4 expect

Read about it

1 Students read article individually and check answer in pairs.

2 Students complete phrases individually. Check answers with the class.

Key
1 dismissal   2 up   3 force   4 surge   5 grounds
6 attitudes   7 from

3 Students write gapped sentences to test their partners on the collocations in Exercise 2.

Listen

1 🔘 **33.1** Play the recording for students to match with picture.

2 **a** Students recall correct words to match with the meanings.

b 🔘 **33.1** Play the recording again for student to check.

Key
1 give up   2 linger on   3 sprightly   4 faculties

Talk about it
Set task as pair work. Students should discuss the pictures based on the questions given. Feed back.

Write about it
Set writing task for class or homework.

Extra activities

1 Write these two sayings on the board:

You're as young as you feel.
You should act your age.

In pairs students discuss the meanings of the sayings and decide which they agree with.

2 Test new vocabulary. Students write anagrams of five new words from the unit to test their partners.

What's the catch?

Summary

Topic: scams and hoaxes

Vocabulary: words with similar meanings

Main task: listening for gist and detailed information

Subsidiary tasks: reading an article; telling a story; writing dialogue or short article

Warmer

Tell students about yourself and ask whether they think you're telling the truth or a lie. How do they know if someone is lying? In pairs they should tell each other five things about themselves, one of which is a lie. How many students guessed the lie?

Procedure

Lead in
Students discuss questions in pairs. Feedback.

Word work
1 a + b Set tasks as individual work and ask students to check in pairs.

Key
1 a con artist   **b** trickster/fraudster   **c** hoaxer
2 con, trick
3 a play a trick/practical joke   **b** commit fraud
c run a scam
4 a fraudulent   **b** tricky

2 Students complete the task individually and check in pairs. Elicit examples of practical jokes, famous con artists, etc.

Key
1 practical jokes   **2** scam   **3** fraud   **4** fraudulent

Listen
1 **34.1** First play the recording for students to listen for general understanding. Ask who the speakers are and what the conversation is about.

Explain the task and let students read through the notes. Play the recording again. Check answers.

Key
1 International Lottery Agency   **2** Parker   **3** second
4 Canadian   **5** 1 million pounds   **6** bank account number
7 transfer   **8** £250   **9** insurance   **10** 5 million

2 **34.1** Play the recording again for students to complete expressions. Elicit other contexts.

Key
1 to inform you   **2** substantial   **3** you through   **4** in order
5 reeling   **6** few details   **7** fortnight   **8** premium

Talk about it
1 Students discuss questions in pairs. Feed back.

Key
Possible answers
1 the caller says she can phone the number back to check
she is transferred to a different department
it's second prize, not first
2 they want her bank details   she didn't enter the lottery herself   they want her to send money

2 Students discuss the message in pairs. Compare answers with the class.

Read about it
1 Ask students to read the article individually. Check understanding.

2 Students find synonyms in the article.

Key
1 wholly   **2** implausible   **3** handed over   **4** notorious
5 confidential

3 In pairs students tell each other about any famous hoaxes.

Write about it
1 Students imagine and plan a hoax in pairs. They should then write an article about the hoax for a magazine. Alternatively, they can write the dialogue between the people involved.

2 The pairs describe their hoaxes and the class votes on the craziest, funniest, most plausible and cleverest.

Extra activity
Dictate these words to the students to practise spelling.

> fraud hoax deception reassuring suspicious notorious implausible prestigious wholly accomplice embarrassed

Elicit the contexts they were used in the unit.

Undercover

Summary

Topic: work, private investigators

Vocabulary: adjectives; collocations

Main task: reading for general and specific understanding

Subsidiary tasks: discussion, writing a PI report

Warmer

Ask students if they can predict what jobs people in the class will have in the future. Can they tell what a person's job is by looking at them? How?

Procedure

Lead in

Students write down professions. They compare lists in pairs and discus questions. Feed back.

Word work

1 Students discuss the meanings of the adjectives. Feed back.

2 Elicit examples from the class of what people like this might do.

Read about it

1 Students discuss pre-reading questions in pairs or as a class.

2 **a + b** Elicit what they would like to find out about in the article. Students then read to check ideas. Feed back.

3 Set task as individual work and put students into pairs to check.

Key

1 F 2 T 3 F 4 F 5 T 6 T

4 Set task as pair work. Feed back. Elicit other contexts.

Key

1 a 2 b 3 b 4 a 5 a 6 b 7 a 8 a 9 b 10 a

5 **a** Students match collocations individually. Check answers with the class.

Key

1 b 2 d 3 f 4 a 5 g 6 e 7 c

b Students test each other in pairs.

Write about it

1 Explain the writing task. The students write their lists individually. They should imagine that they are hiring a PI to check up on someone – husband, wife, employee, suspected criminal, etc.

2 Students exchange lists. Now they imagine they are the PI who has tailed the person and must write the report. To do this they should use the list and their imagination.

Extra activities

1 Students read the text again and write a summary of the article in no more than 100 words.

2 Students play 'Twenty Questions' in pairs choosing unusual jobs. Alternatively, they give the class five pieces of information about their jobs for others to guess what they do.

3 Students write anagrams of eight of the adjectives from the unit for their partners to solve.

Dangerous fun

Summary

Topic: risk taking; health and safety

Vocabulary: expressions for a discursive essay

Main task: writing a discursive essay

Subsidiary tasks: discussion; reading an article

Warmer

Write *Don't try this at home!* on the board and elicit where this message might be seen (before certain TV shows). Ask for names of such programmes and examples of what the shows are about.

Procedure

Lead in

Students discuss questions in pairs. Feed back.

Read about it

1 Set reading task for individual work and ask students to check answers in pairs.

Key

1 Presenters talk about cars and take part in tests and races.
2 They enjoy it because they can't have the experience themselves.
3 One of the a presenters was involved in a serious crash.
4 It may be stopped or its content changed because some people think it is not right to show such dangerous activities on TV.
5 He/She thinks the programme should continue as it is and that risk is up to the individual.

---

2 Students work together to find words in text.

Key

1 fans   **2** the powers that be   **3** banned
4 called into question   **5** outrageous   **6** issues
7 experience a vicarious thrill   **8** toned down

Talk about it

1 Students prepare ideas for opposing point of view in pairs and feed back to the class.

2 Students explain and defend their own points of view. Alternatively, they can be given a point of view that they have to defend.

Write about it

1 Elicit ways of expressing contrasting opinions and information. Students complete task individually. Feed back.

2 Read through the phrases and give students time to write follow up sentences. Write up some of the students' answers on the board.

3 Set writing task for homework.

Extra activities

1 Write these topics on the board and ask students to choose one and talk about it for two minutes in small groups.

---

fast driving   smoking   the environment
public transport   discipline in school

---

2 Elicit the names of some extreme sports. Students plan and write a short advertisement for one of these sports to go in a college magazine.

3 Put students into pairs and give each pair a piece of paper with the statement *We are less free today than twenty years ago.* at the top. Students have a written conversation discussing the statement. Feed back.

Leave those
kids alone

Summary

Topic: childhood

Vocabulary: word building; expressions for giving opinions

Main task: assessing and discussing modern school rules

Subsidiary tasks: reading an article for gist; writing a description

Warmer

Describe one of your memories of your experience at primary school. Elicit memories from the class. If necessary, write on prompts on the board: *food*, *friends*, *teachers*, *accidents*, etc.

Procedure

Lead in

Students discuss questions in pairs. Feed back. Do all the students describe similar experiences?

Read about it

1 Students read article. Elicit a summary sentence. Students then match the points of view and the comments.

Key

1 B   2 A   3 B   4 B   5 B   6 A   7 B

Word work

1 Set tasks as individual work and ask students to check in pairs.

Key

nouns: applause   implementation   imposition   instigation   interference   ridicule   concern   contribution   protection   welcome
same form: ridicule   concern   welcome

2 Set task as individual work and ask students to check in pairs.

Key

1 ridicule   2 contribution   3 imposed, implement
4 applauded   5 instigated

Talk about it

1 Read through the rules with the class. Compare ideas.

2 Set task as pair work. Feed back and compare ideas with the class.

3 Read through the useful language. Students discuss the questions in pairs and compare their ideas with the rest of the class.

Write about it

Set writing task for class or homework.

Extra activity

In pairs students imagine a school either in the year 2050 or in the year 1950. They write a set of school rules for this school. They should include:

- Students must …
- Students must not …

What's the score?

Summary

Topic: films; film scores

Vocabulary: words with similar meanings

Main task: listening to a synopsis for detailed information

Subsidiary tasks: discussion; writing a synopsis

Warmer

Ask students about the most recent film they've seen. Ask what they can remember about the actors, scenery, special effects and music. Give them the words *score* and *soundtrack*.

Procedure

Lead in

1 Students discuss questions in pairs. Feed back.

2 Students write names of films for different categories. Feed back.

Word work

Set task for individual work and ask students to check in pairs. Feed back. If necessary, check understanding of differences in meanings.

Key
1 b   2 a   3 d   4 b   5 c   6 c

Listen

1 Students discuss questions in small groups. Feed back.

2 🔘 **38.1** Explain the task. Give time for students to read through the names and the people. Play the recording for students to complete the matching task. Feed back.

Key
1 c   2 e   3 a   4 b   5 f   6 d

3 🔘 **38.1** Set task as individual work. Play the recording again for students to check answers. Feed back. Check meanings by asking for examples of different contexts.

Key
1 embezzles   2 isolated   3 adjacent   4 bedridden
5 traps   6 shadowy   7 horrified   8 distract   9 basement
10 mummified   11 suspicious   12 rage   13 identity

Write about it

1 🔘 **38.2** Ask students if they have seen any silent movies. Check they know how the music was added to the film (an organ was played in the cinema as the film was being shown). Explain that they are going to hear some of this music. They should match the themes. Play the recording. Ask for answers.

2 Elicit that the synopsis is written in present tenses. Students choose one piece of music and discuss a possible story in pairs. They then write a short synopsis.

Extra activities

1 Do a soundtrack quiz. Ask students to write down five songs associated with films to test their partners.

2 Use this text on Bernard Herrmann for a reading comprehension.

> Bernard Herrmann wrote the scores for many famous films, including *Citizen Kane* but is perhaps most well known for his work with Alfred Hitchcock, in particular for his film score for the ground breaking horror film of 1960, *Psycho*. There have been three sequels and a remake but the original is still widely considered to be the best not least due to Herrmann's amazing film score. It is said that Herrmann actually ignored Hitchcock's specific instructions regarding the music and came up with a haunting masterpiece that depends solely on strings; violins and cellos. The strings convey everything that Hitchcock wanted to show in his film – dread, longing, regret, fear. As with many fine films, the score is an integral part of the whole cinematic experience.

1 How many *Psycho* films are there altogether? (5)

2 Which is considered the best? (the original/first one)

3 What was Bernard Herrmann's job? (composer)

4 What instruments did he use in the film score for *Psycho*? (violins/cellos)

5 Had he and Hitchcock agreed on this beforehand? (no)

Let it all **out**

Summary

Topic: showing emotion

Vocabulary: idioms and colloquial expressions

Main task: reading for general and specific understanding

Subsidiary tasks: discussion; writing a comment for a website

Warmer

Draw two faces on the board – one smiling, one frowning. Brainstorm as many words as possible associated with the two. Add tears to the two faces. Brainstorm again. Add frown lines to the second face. Continue.

Procedure

Lead in

Students discuss questions in pairs. Feed back.

Word work

1 Students complete task individually and check in pairs. Feed back. Check understanding.

Key

L: creased up   to be in fits   get the giggles
A: lose it   blow your top   freak out   burst a blood vessel
have a good rant
E: I could've died
S: get it off your chest   show your true colours
wear your heart on your sleeve

2 Explain the task. In pairs one student gives the other a phrase. The other student must then describe a situation to illustrate it. E.g. *creased up – Yesterday Mike was showing off on his bicycle and he fell off. I creased up!* Students complete the task. Feed back.

Talk about it

Students discuss questions in pairs. Feed back.

Read about it

1 Students do the task individually and check in pairs. Feed back.

Key

1 well up   have a good cry   moist-eyed   solitary tear
full-on blubbing   shed a tear   cried openly   weeping
turn on the waterworks
2 guy   man   males   masculinity   a man's man   manly

2 Ask students to correct any false statements and underline parts of the text that give them the information.

Key

1 F   **2** F   **3** T   **4** T   **5** T   **6** T

Write about it

Set writing task for class or homework.

Extra activity

1 Students copy different paragraphs from the article and leave gaps for different words. They exchange texts with their partners and complete the gaps.

2 Test students on the new vocabulary by giving first part of phrases to elicit full phrase. Alternatively, get students to make cards with the different parts of the expressions on different cards, turn them face down and play a memory matching game (pelmanism)

Shopped out

Summary

Topic: shopping

Vocabulary: phrases used in report writing

Main task: writing a report

Subsidiary tasks: discussion, read a report

Warmer

Put students into pairs and give them two minutes to write down as many different shops as they can. Which pair has the most?

Procedure

Lead in

1 Students discuss questions in pairs. Feed back.

2 Students complete questionnaire individually and compare answers with partner. Feed back.

3 Students the pictures in pairs. Feed back.

Word work

Students complete task individually and check answers in pairs. Feed back.

Read about it

1 Ask students their opinions of local shopping malls/ centres.

Students read the report and discuss answers as a class.

Key

1 modern design   simple lay out   impression of space
cleanliness   range of shops   restaurants
amount of parking space
2 not enough Mall maps   not enough Mall staff available
not enough lifts   no coffee shop
not enough toilet facilities   cost of parking high
3 The recommendations don't address current high cost of parking/extra lifts.

2 Students work in pairs to find verbs and phrases.

Key

questions were asked
most of those questioned
(they) generally found
Many mentioned
was also praised
a number of people expressed a desire for
a request was also made
it was also noted
most considered the parking fees excessive
maps should be displayed

The passive is often used in survey reports because it is impersonal and avoids the repeated use of *the people*. Occasional use of the active voice provides variety.

3 Students find formal equivalents and check with partners. Feed back.

Key

1 address   **2** advisable   **3** feasible   **4** forseeable future
5 facilitate

4 Students underline phrases where the words occur in the report. These phrases can later be used in the writing task.

Key

1 the aim of this report is to
2 it is based on a survey
3 questions were asked concerning
4 most of those questioned
5 a number of people expressed a desire
6 the vast majority of those surveyed
7 However, a significant number mentioned
8 it was also noted by

Write about it

1 Read through the report phrases in *Read about it* Exercise 4 with students and then explain writing task. Students work in pairs to discuss an imaginary mall.

2 Students write the report individually. Remind them of the important points.

Extra activity

Set up a role play. In pairs students take it in turns to be one of the surveyors at the entrance to Tyndell Shopping Mall or a shopper being questioned. Give them time to write the questions they are going to ask. The shoppers can choose their persona – teenager, young married person, retired/ elderly, etc. Students complete role plays. Feed back.

Published by
DELTA PUBLISHING
Quince Cottage
Hoe Lane
Peaslake
Surrey GU5 9SW
England

www.deltapublishing.co.uk

First published 2009

ISBN 978-1-905085-27-9

Edited by Tanya Whatling
Designed by Christine Cox
Printed by Halstan & Co., Amersham, Bucks, England